The Afterlife

For Alex

THE AFTERLIFE

ANTHONY WILSON

with good wishes

Anthony

Oct 19.

First published in 2019 by
Worple Press
Achill Sound, 2b Dry Hill Road
Tonbridge
Kent TN9 1LX.
www.worplepress.co.uk

Printed by imprintdigital
Upton Pyne, Exeter
www.imprintdigital.com

Typeset and cover design by narrator typesetters and designers
www.narrator.me.uk
info@narrator.me.uk
033 022 300 39

ISBN: 978-1-905208-42-5

for Tatty

Thaw

Now we are in the darkness
we know nothing but the search
for rays we cannot gaze into, as,

on grey days, we know their heat
from how the frost retreats
to green behind a wave of light.

Contents

But how much survives? How much of any one of us survives?

– John Ashbery

Part One

Teaching Writing Theory

On Tuesday I discovered whether my cancer
had returned. Later I discussed teaching writing
to six-year-olds. We spun our arms
like windmills, then made chopstick-motions
with our fingers mirroring the motor control
functions we daily take for granted
even less think about as we stare at the page.
We looked at motivational theory. Taxonomies
and heuristics jammed the white-board,
a cacophony of formulations we all wanted
to witness taking flight. During self-study,
I watched students tap-tapping at mobiles
and tablets, all the while sustaining complex
discussions about pedagogy and dress codes
for their forthcoming Christmas parties.
If they were nervous of the outcome
of their assignments, none of them showed it.

What I Should be Feeling

rips into the lullaby of my heart
somewhere in the middle of the chord change
of the disabled boy's mother being shown
her son's new soft-furnished bedroom.
If I could stop buying collections of poems
and if I had time to read them
none of this would matter. We are a little
family, protected by nothing more than prayer,
the inheritance of ancestors we know through stories
such as how we came by this armchair
or that particular angle of chin.
The relentless interactivity of the world
refuses to let us sleep or make dreams
at the pace we desire; it mistakes
my outstretched hand as a vote in its favour,
silent and fast as the equipment
held in it, registering mild complaint
or pause as identical.
Nothing I ever say will recreate the magic
of the pathologist's look of awe on completing
the face of a girl she is now equal to.
Rediscover my fingers stretching
towards you, even as you giggle
at this chat-show audience applauding its own surprise.

Slow Weather

Each of us differently afraid
of what the other might not say,

there is no telling, this January afternoon,
what will become of us pulling

at products our eyes taste
before we do. The day, illuminated

and indifferent, like any other, a little sad,
perhaps, the drizzle with something of Madrid

in it, or Milan, but unique as our nostrils,
and open as them to the uneasy

and unseen air we push through,
the procession of our dutiful trolleys somehow

grand and illustrious, filled with exciting cheeses.
Looking for reasons to part before greeting,

alert as collies at dipping time,
there is nothing which cannot be subsumed

into courtly anecdote or gossip
about those we avoid in public,

that very sense of the public governing
this exchange of nods nobody

sees but us. Wishing
each other well via news of unnamed colleagues,

we are released back to ourselves,
all choice open before us

from donuts to joint-pain remedies,
our decisions invisible as charity.

On Losing the Ability to Sleep

I have not felt desired by you
in years. When was the last time
you curled your body into mine,
placed your hand on my forehead?
I have forgotten when you greeted me
wearing nothing but a 'Hello Horny'
T shirt, as when you first moved in.
You vowed to soothe my night sweats,
but when morning arrived your promises
vanished. Can I not trust you even
for basic courtesy? You appear
in the bath and on motorways!
You call me out of meetings,
or when I am speaking
with my children. How dare you.
Remember how you wooed me
with your simplicity? You carried
then unpacked my bags.
Though your chat-up lines were ancient
I could have killed for your smile.

To Spring

Some days I stare at the distance
and others it comes to me
dragging me into its pull

splicing the future
answerable to no one
dogged cur

surefooted reptile of thought.
Attempting resistance is futile.
Ditto, anger. Best to ride out its

spiral in silence, never
anticipation. Again I am snared,
down here on my island of one.

In Oregon

When I am on my deathbed
recalling life-changing art
this is the reading I will keep.
One filthy night in Bodmin:
the soddenness in our bones,
rain on the slates and teacups,
as Anthony spoke about Melville
and Matthew suicide and fire.
We did not 'wait five more minutes';
the car park did not burst
with a coach trip. We were there,
we can say it, to hear Anthony pull
Berryman from memory,
warmth and mutual respect
blanket and shield to the elements,
two voices and hail on the roof,
the bookstall groaning behind them.
When Matthew invited us to stay with him,
he explained we were *already* in Oregon,
I mean it—I would love it—you and all your dogs.

British Teeth

If I were not here writing
I would be here writing
my life as a spy:
those cabs to moonlit airfields,
the lovers and second-rate traffickers
slain by my charm and knife;
my diet of cashews and vodka,
my knack of knowing
when to twist and when to quit,
invariably in plain view,
like the nose on my face
or the voice I was born with,
though modified by travel
and schooling, bartering
with ease on all continents,
sometimes for one for the road,
and others my life, the one I lived,
not this other one, inside my head,
taking shape in front of me,
chewing at all that white space.

Mornings in Paradise

Each morning we make our way
through the ghost resort to our beach
with no one on it. It's a creaking, listing
curio of a thing in monumental bamboo,
empty since the bombs but for a squatting
caretaker who hangs his washing neatly
on a line from his hut to the derelict gents.
Overnight, Berni says, the jetty-wood disappeared,
the islanders reclaiming it for their houses.
This was after the first wave, she tells us,
just bonfires and guitars, *before the money*.
Now all that has gone. Except for those brothers
lighting fireworks in their hands,
their daredevil cackling, the very English way
they yelled 'Whoosh!' and collapsed giggling.

She came here for love, she tells us,
the evidence of which we eat in Madé's gnocchi,
and banana pancakes reinventing sweetness.
Cockerels wake us around four, I guess, one of them
leaving a question mark at the climax of each cry.
We wait without touching for the imam to start.
He begins a little bossily, sometimes sounding shy,
as if giving stream of consciousness advice, hardly
a *call* to anything, more muttered reminiscence.
His reticence reminds me of those gamelan players
picking up their hammers and resuming
their performance without looking at each other,
the sudden look of mortality in their eyes
as they sit cross-legged checking their phones.

Balinese Surfers

Whooping joy
at each other's skill,
they hurtle on breaks,
dodging the bobbing coconuts
and detritus—
flip flops, dishcloths, tampons—
from half-way round the globe.
The colour of teak.
Nerveless–glistening,
Elvis–quiffed,
they holler and yodel,
high-fiving and applauding
in the collapsing surf
which froths like soda
poured too fast
into a glass,
imprinting itself on the sand
with pale fizz as it dies.

Thinking Outside

It is twilight in Cornwall. Wedding guests
and your kids maze between us,
the air not midge-thick, but promising to be.
As ceilidh tunes start practising themselves
you toss me your theory of Calvinist football,
toe-the-line, not-to-lose pragmatism wrapping
itself like a trap around the idea of *playing*,
depression as the last site of liberation:
'We haven't *dissected* anger yet,
let alone acknowledged it's there.'
At the back stick I nod it across
for you to slide-rule the winning link
between MacDiarmid and Fergie's Aberdeen,
their genius of excess without money.
From here to the dance floor is pure breeze,
the Big Seven, MacCaig in a pub in Leith,
his greatness sloshing out of him like whisky.
Joined by our wives we go for civilized,
your kids and ours, job histories, teaching.
A bairn, your third, is lolling-perched wide-eyed,
momentarily sated. ('I'm not expecting help,
it's fine.') Toasting the damage we'll do next time
to an innocent malt and (who knows? why not?)
on the back of that a grant to change the world,
we go back to them, shadowed on the lawn,
our high wires wobbling, not expecting help.

Poem Beginning With a Line by John Ash

What do I do? I look out the window,
reflected in Victorian facades,
at the terrible dusk, which even now
seeps into my bones like a chemical injection
or wave of depression on coming
across an especially tedious journal of educational research.
The day had promised so much, Schuyler says;
it held so little, or was it I who in asking
too much received less than I deserved?
A brunch with brilliant friends, cleansing
the vegetable patch and ditto my groaning bookshelves,
most of which I will not miss: pleasures of flesh
and mind which are the author of each other.
How else does one daydream phrases
like 'stupefying sunlight' but mulching
rotted marrow flowers? How else tell the labour
of the same but in silence? Tonight I may walk
and capture the book-lined study where a woman
sits working. For a moment I will stare
right into her, aware that all she sees is mirror,
not me watching her with pity and a shrug
at the silence, the kind that is a hum,
somewhere in the valley a railway and somewhere
crossing that a motorway, with its halogen and its orange.

The Barchester Chronicles

A friend said to think of them as campus:
'like *The Wire* without the drugs.'
Each night I drift off to Maggie Steed's
Mrs Baxter, amazed at the miracle
of making me love what I believed I hated
but never read during my degree in The Smiths,
their intrigue fresher than Watergate,
those far-off bishops and clerics slicing
each other's careers without a second thought.

How modern; how prophetic; how History:
another of Maggie's great roles—Myra Beamish's hand
through a window at a party, everyone too stoned
to notice; professors shagging their students,
the booze and smoking during meetings,
how quaint it all seems, *pas de deux* arguments
of principle and procedure laced with ganja and Marx.
I'd call it work, learning all this, but it isn't.
Thanks to yours, they become people, knowable.

Staffroom, Summer, 2015

I

A Life Without Levels poster hanging by one pin
groups children as emerging, developing, secure
or having mastery, for example 'writing in different contexts'.
They should try it in here, where silence collects
under chairs round the room's outskirts
like uncles at a funeral, sure of their place
and distrustful of change. A tin of brownies
squares up to a gift set of hand creams
on the boardroom-sized table: *Help yourselves!*
I wonder what they *would* write given the chance,
given the freedom, and if that's even what they'd call it,
a blank sheet and light enough with just the fridge,
and the urn steaming, almost like home.
Plus the Lottery's come on brilliantly, £990 for a yurt
so they can learn to cook outdoors and build fires
the old-fashioned way, or even camp out and marvel
at stars, the uncluttered, unlearnable stars.

II

Or this, forty minutes and a world away,
views across the estuary from the all-age canteen
Jamie Oliver would die for. I mooch about the library
which is a foyer and think I'm in Silicon Valley,
all lime green sofas, water coolers and purring phones.
Apparently there isn't an actual room they call their own,
hot-desking with the kids on iPads handed out like sweets
at the front desk like a rampart. Tomorrow I'll travel
back through time to when school was a house
in a village, where no one meets to sit in a room
smaller than this table, but where there are always biscuits.
Deliberately without noticing I find I'm next to POETRY:
Roald Dahl's nonsense props *Rain-Charm for The Duchy*
and a how-to creative writing last taken out in never.
I'm not going anywhere, so lose this hour for years
relearning salmon, their micro-sensitive spawning,
the river a slingshot down the hill, silent and unvisited.

From a Chalkface

'There's a very interesting reason why a prince could not turn into a frog. It's statistically too improbable.' – Richard Dawkins

Strata, I wonder what you'd make of us
    searching your map online and enlarging

      with our fingers your fossilised layers,
        their thickness, dip and geometry

pulsing and alive like an excited frontal lobe
    at the moment of discovering

      some of them were younger.
        We can conjure with a flick

what took you an age to witness—
    including the workings of these minds;

      their unicorn-allowing chemistry is a fault line
        in the rational. Rather like the odds

you'd find on a blacksmith by that name
    marrying one of the same,

      their son schooled in the village.

Utterance Dusk

I cannot write about clouds
so I write about clouds
chasing me across this pasture
where I once ran as a boy.

The clouds do not remember:
they were the same clouds,
they were entirely different,
it makes no difference.

I am not angry with the clouds,
they owe me nothing.

Calling me by name, the clouds
are their own answer, a dream
at walking pace I cannot recall.

Three Pieces (Poem Beginning With a Line by Yehuda Amichai)

The rain is my home
    It wraps its arms around me
    whispering words of hope
The rain is falling
    It greets me with a kiss
Three times it kisses me
    a mother sending her child
    to be good at school
The rain is kind
    It knows my name
It is not cold
    It buys me a new coat
It stays to water my garden
    The rain comes to me
as a memory of one boy
punching another
    but this soon ceases
The rain promises
    it will never leave
It leaves me
    by the river into which it flows
There are ducks there
and children throwing bread
    shouting Ducks!

    ★

I walk in the rain
It is raining
    My head is wet
    my unprotected head
    my only protection

I am happy to be
in the rain happy
    as it slides
      from my face.

★

I have become the rain
    Its bones are mine
    supple and soft
    in the wind
I turn this way and that
    among its fine rods
I do not deserve it
    I have no shadow
I long to become one
    with the rain
I do not understand
    who the rain wants me to be
It takes my hand
    I follow saying yes
The rain is in my arms
    I am in the arms of the rain
I walk in its wandering voice
    far from myself
    I am home.

Part Two

The Afterlife

By the time you accepted you were ill
and began receiving visitors

it was too late
for the doctors to intervene

on your ravaged liver.
It was December, and freezing.

That first visit you told me in your kitchen,
I have wasted my life.

I have missed the childhoods of my children,
and for what?

I thought of all the emails
you had sent with a time stamp of midnight

or three in the morning,
just one more request, one more idea

before bed.
And what about you, how are you, your children,

you said. They're so lucky
to have had you all these years.

Are they well?
You shared with them your afterlife,

something I won't get to do,
it makes me angry.

The All-Clear

Dear Em, I miss you in my bones.
It's filthy today, grey November downpour, unmoving clouds.

The kind of day you'd sneak in uninvited and set about
the kitchen making pancakes and drop scones muttering
        obscenities

you pretended the children could not hear or did not
        understand.
Or storm in, exhausted by teachers too slow to keep up
        with you

frightened you might be right about the 'unbelievably bad
        writing' of Jane Austen.
I lost an uncle in September. You'd have liked him. You
        shared a love

of language and of friends, plummeting from laughter into
        shyness
and to hurt within a glance or unkind word you'd use to cut

both ways without mercy. One night before a funeral he
        took me to one side
to tell me I had conquered myself, a riddle I'm still
        puzzling over.

I'd like to report change in the world you'd be happy with,
but wince at the thought of it, knowing already your volley

of reprimand for living 'so fucking safely'. I know, too,
your instant regret, brownies left on the doorstep,

another lunch for free with 'borrowed' ingredients
but grateful all the same, like receiving books we'd lent as
   presents,

your afterthought reviews somehow the main show in
   plain sight.
Ben says the last time you came over you brought cake.

A more depleted flan it was hard to imagine. But it *was*
   delicious,
maybe your best, even if we did exchange mere syllables.

You were pretty much silent, keeping to the edge of the room
like me with my chemo-head, though for different reasons
   allergic

to the others. God knows what we talked about, though I
   flatter myself
to remember you smiled. 'I'm more used to writing poems
   about me.'

What you won't know, of course, is my consultant gave
   me the all-clear
that very morning. We came home, had some lunch, I slept,

then wrote a while before the phone went. A day pretty
   much like today
except it contained you, somewhere, breathing.

The True Story of the Night they Told me I was Cured

We were watching *CSI Miami* when the phone went,
to congratulate me, you said. Dishes lay at our feet,
penne with a blood-dark sauce, which we wolfed.
I had stayed off the wine because the doctors warned my body
wasn't ready for it.
                 As we digest the news
we scramble for coats, hats and scarves, anything to shut out
the cold which now grips us as we drive across town
to where the news lies like a crime scene
but with nothing to see, nothing you could call tangible,
like evidence.

There are Days

There are days I lose to knowing
it has come back.

An ache in my back, a run of night sweats.
Then nothing.

I am me again, climbing out of bed
to make the tea where I watch blue tits stab

the feeder,
pausing sometimes.

This happened, it is still happening,
it is over, it will never be over.

There it is again, my breath,
that stabbing, it's back.

Death Shelf

And for some reason
we asked about keeping orchids,

how you stop them dying
once they lose their leaves.

Death shelf, you said. You need a death shelf.
And you showed us your death shelf,

the wrinkled tendrils like grey fingers
trying to reach out of earth,

three of them, denuded, potted, in a row.
A north facing window. It has to face north

you said. A cup of water
once a week, and suddenly it all happens.

The Last Time I Saw Mary

The last time I saw Mary
was in her kitchen, September sunlight, the door open to
     her garden.

She gave me a tutorial
on my book, warning me not to be meretricious.

Your faith, she said, don't be afraid
of it. It is who you are.

She was skinny by then, her grey hair
in a bob, like a girl's.

Shuffling in her slippers she made coffee
and brought waffles.

The Dutch balance these on their cups
and watch them deliquesce

into the hot liquid, she said. So sweet.
To an English person, their name is unpronounceable.

I said, I think you can buy them in Lidl now.
They cost nothing.

Chicken and Almond Soup

I skinned a finger of ginger,
grated and set it to fry,
peeled a sweet potato,
two carrots, diced,
and added them to the pan
with a teaspoon of cumin,
a chicken thigh, and precisely
twenty twists of pepper,
a little stock to keep
from sticking. I covered
and let it sweat, and when the thigh
was brown, shredded
and sent it back to the pan
with the stock, some coconut
and a mound of ground almonds,
with mustard to taste.
Bringing to the boil
I pulverized and let it cool,
then poured into pots
I'd bought specially,
five of them in all,
more than a person
could stomach, their
hard lids unblinking.
I wrapped them in ice
and set off around four
through the dusk and crowds
of head-bowed shoppers
and students in T shirts
though it was winter,
oblivious to the cold.

Sitting With Your Body

When the others had gone
we sat with your body for a while
and watched you pass over
from person to body, watched you
become blue, then grey, then ivory,
then grey again, the cave of your ribs
no longer heaving, and Tatty stroked
your shoulder as if comforting
a child who was poorly and hadn't slept,
all the while watching your stillness,
finally you were still, as though present,
then we kissed your ice forehead
and found our coats and walked
across the common to eat with the others.

Part Three

To a Notebook

All summer long the lorries have passed
My window taking earth from one end
Of the street to the other, on an eternal quest
For silence and rest.   Now Joe brings
His radio and sets up shop right outside,
All the hits I used to know and now resent
For filling this moment with noise
I did not ask for.   The house that took till
October to build is now taking till December.
I sat for so long listening to trucks beeping-
Reversing I no longer hear them (not true).
It's amazing I go to church: for a non-joiner
Like me, a miracle.   I'm there to have my
Edges knocked off, plus knock those I slowly
Learn to love. After a week of people,
Silence.   The breeze finding its voice
Like rain on apple leaves but without rain,
So prolific with windfalls this year,
We hear them thud and roll from the house,
The territorial robin that has sung all summer
Suddenly clearer than thought while I make
Lists for eggs and books I want to have read,
This paper, scratchy yet smooth, is the best—
Since when?—France, probably (maybe
All the answers are France).   The worst part
Is starting, but then you know that already.
Twitter can't keep up with me, nor I
With it: help me, someone, understand
Why I need to applaud your cake.
The delicious loneliness of staying
In a town where no one speaks English,
The rain never more alive than when

I lay awake listening to dawn inch closer
Through the fizzing traffic.   Only a week ago
Automated hosepipes like cicadas sprayed
In sunshine ('The Cathedral is not a happy place,'
Said—not telling). Then blue tits invaded
The apple tree after a summer away,
A silent V of geese arrows across
Ochre-orange clouds, my heart a shipwreck
To follow their progress.   I sleep badly
And make others do the same. I try
To sleep in the day, but no. At school
We scored the girls, hair, smile, body parts,
Gait, how long they spent chatting
With seniors we hated for their access
And punishments when the girls weren't
Looking.   This pen, so scratchy yet smooth,
Some days I think I will use it forever.
I listen to a podcast and put away summer
Shirts, fold sheets and think of you
And Sweden, the horns of ships in the sound
We only saw from the upstairs balcony,
Remembering suddenly both my children
Live on separate continents.   I should call
To see if they are safe. The day
Longs for toast, so I make some
While not listening to the radio. Is it
Lengthening, the day, even as it stretches
Towards winter?   Taking Shim to the airport
We talked about the Spurs game. Suddenly
It was time to go and we had a deep hug.
Always the same pricking of my eyes
In the twenty yards between check-in
And the door. I miss him already.
Shall I put 'Weinstein' to make my poem
More googleable? The problem is my ego,

Not his.   In the days before satnav
I would drive out to watch failing teachers
And talk them through their options
Of how to re-order their stationery.
All those Beths and Emilys I stopped crying
To listen to what they knew anyway.
Who is this 'God'? a poet on Facebook says.
(I wasn't being personal.)   When sun
Pierces the gunmetal and lifts the field
Below it to a new kind of green,
Or when trees shed everything in a night
(Like last night) to reveal nests, long
Abandoned, in forks between bare branches,
Or when a sudden gust of hope bounces
Round the corner in the form of a child
Carrying a balloon on a string, that's
When I know He or It (it?) or She
Hasn't left me, or I Him/Her. I'm not
Sure which way round it's supposed to be.
        I used to play cricket with men who used
'Winter' as a verb. 'How have you wintered?'
'Have you wintered well?' I hope I will.
The thought of another plunge scares me.
A jet drifts through its tuning fork tones
And takes forever to cross the sky.
I tried so hard to pay attention
In maths, I think it nearly killed me
(Not to mention my poor teachers).
My parents are still on good terms
With the tutor who came, sweating,
Each week to try and rescue me.
Richard, he was called. I hope he has
Forgiven me by now, so much easier
Than forgiving yourself.   One, Mr Wigam,
Read ghost stories to us at the end

Of each term, the only maths I remember.
'You could land Concorde on that pencil,
Wilson, it's so thick—just like you.'
It was a maths teacher, too, who told me
I was 'polytechnic material', even though
He'd never spoken to me before (though
He *had* taught my father—probably wearing
The same suit).   I wonder if that is why
I do this, scratch around, as at the crease
When it is swinging, looking for words
To remember which in the end are new ways
Of being silent? I'd happily shoot all of them
Were they not dead already.   English was where
They listened, having prompted us to talk.
Such a revolution, that, that we brought
Things to say. Most of us didn't, but liked
Trying anyway, even if 'Pike' wasn't a Nazi
As one boy kept insisting.   Or that other,
Justin, not yet out, who muttered 'Freud'
Each time the class fell silent
Or when Borton ran out of things to say.
Not a bad way of getting through school,
I thought, to find hilarious the private joke
No one else could see and which had no point
Except for the time we did Lawrence,
And Borton called him out on it, inviting
An explanation. Justin bloomed pinker
Than the cherry blossom he was describing.
I thought: now *that* was a piece of teaching.

        This paper, so—what, exactly? Blank
Is what comes to mind, that perfect state
I long for at the end of each day,
Nothing left on the pitch as the athletes say,
No one needing forgiving, including me by me,
Before dreams with the absorbency

Of glass and the texture of freshly
Applied paint, like the lavatory paper
They handed out at school.   This paper:
I dragged my family across Stockholm
To find it and don't regret it for a second,
As much of a revelation as finding Degas
For the first time with Mart on Interrail
During our shorts and string vest phase.
'If we're in a one horse town,' he said,
'We'll go and look at the horse.'
I learned more about sculpture and dance
In all my half hours busking with him
Than from a thousand books. He taught:
You show up and it happens; the only rule:
Tune up first, then let them have it,
Even the man spitting abuse and Mahler
From his window in Strasbourg.
Desperate and ashamed, defeated
And afraid, angry and denied, I know
You'd like to scream like a sigh, like a sigh.

Men on scaffolding glint in high-vis gilets,
Walking like men walk here on earth,
Not looking up. A family business
Of sparrows goes about its business
In the hedge. Books arrive from the library,
Fresher than fish. The fat robin ignores
The thin robin next to it in the feeder.

By this time tomorrow I will be in Cornwall
Watching noun phrases and lining up.
World supplies of gunk make torrents
In ducts behind my face. (Still not sure
About this Mango Berocca.) These easy-
Peel tangerines are not easy-peel tangerines.
An afternoon by the fire, jotting notebook
Jottings, occasionally pausing to read,

White light on the white houses opposite.
(Would Woolf have given us *The Waves*
Had she played on Twitter?)   The visit
Wasn't a failure, but we failing to spot
What lay in front of us (the birdsong the same
But different) in the admiring diary of the tourist.
This is being stored somewhere.
Not me, but then that has ceased to be the point.
Sadly.   Today will have to do, my I more plural
By the minute, clamouring for my attention
While I just—wasn't Nadine's chair
A fixture only a year ago? Where
Has it gone to now? Did I answer Hermione's email
About wellies?   One day someone will tell me,
Ordering me before the beak, as at school,
To be caned (without the cane) for inserting x
After my name in a hurry to be nice,
Nothing more to it than the equivalent
Of a shrug. You close down our social spaces
And this is what happens, no one talks
Any more, yet expects everything done
Yesterday. (I don't think I did answer her,
Perhaps I am safe.)   *Whilst of course*
There was a chemical story to my depression
Sounds mainly as though said depression
Might still be with us or at least a daily fight
(I hate that word) to ward it off.
Can you? By prayer? Or swimming?

    My public I's don't help. Nor yours,
The very reason I left Facebook, somewhere
Between the couple up to their ears in bubble bath
And the artist making copies of Grand Masters
Explaining *why* on a video because he was paid.
That GIF of Viggo Mortensen was funny
But I am Bored—Bored!—of The Rings.

Nadine waved to me across the traffic,
But it was not Nadine. Books I was given
During cancer just won the Nobel Prize,
Which goes to show, life is all about the timing.
I walked into a field and heard nothing
But the field. I walked into a meeting
And heard nothing but the meeting.
(Meeting is the last thing it was.)
I thought I was saying goodbye,
But feel as though I am saying hello.
      Children, where are you? Are you well?
I hope so. I pray for it each day.
Wan light, October light, I love you
Even though too soon you are November
And charcoal, even at 7.40, twenty to eight,
Big hand hiding the little hand, becoming
One hand, frozen stroke on the clock face,
Time rolling away from me like an apple
Across the kitchen table.   But I like
How I live, even if my decisions not to use
Royal Mail and make calls with microchips
Fashioned by children paid a pittance
Prick my conscience where it hurts,
Which is here, in the silent heart
I guard from everyone but you,
Blank friend, who receives me daily
Without fail or frowning, without question,
Even when I try inks just the once before
Abandoning them.   What is happiness?
A long pile of words, tied together
With string and effort. Every day
You take something and stretch it out,
Like a dog after a long walk by the sea.
I want to be by the sea but instead
Have this kitchen clock: sometimes

What you know is what you make up.
Still, this skateboarding cat will not write
The poem by itself. We will all have to chip in.
        God comes to you disguised as your life
I read the other day. It may be true,
If life is what you are left with once
You've dealt with how you come to *know*
Is via pain (for me, at least), the loss
Of what doesn't bring life. Recursive
And circuitous, you grab it (Him?) and it (She?)
Goes. Sit still with everything broken
About you and He's there.   Sometimes
I get so bored of talking about myself
I invent poetry magazines to appear in,
Then list them on my CV, passports
To sit around in meetings while others
Explain their plans for overseas adventures
And writing in forbidden languages.
Not my strongest suit, and, if we're honest,
Not theirs. But still. This is how the world
Now works, and always has, more's the pity.
        A leaf just blew by my window.
Quite high for a leaf, I thought.
A plank leans against the house opposite,
As if holding it up, or pretending to.
Remind me, how much Lemsip is dangerous?
(I waited till my fifties to start taking care of my teeth.
My toothpaste contains plastic beads
That are killing the whales. Jean says
There is a platform of them five miles wide
In the Pacific. Note to self: Be Better.)
        This pencil, so grey, so rare, someone's
Photo of their amazing life. I have played
Tennis with aristocrats, while secretly combatting
My need to be liked. (I don't think it showed.)

44

Notebook, what are you adding, adoring?
Like a tourist gazing up at a cathedral
But not venturing into it, I am aware
Of my need to repent, as after a drunken toast
I call to mind how much I missed with my words,
Even those I wanted to use in front of those
I loved, and how next time (will there be one?)
Will need to raise its game.   At school
You could not be both oarsman and batter,
Disco and indie, science and art, CU and normal.
God was an angry housemaster
Out to stop you having fun, and who did: Lent,
A whole term named after it, never explained.
Wild light, raking light, I have seen you before,
But never like today, *that will not come again.*

    I waited till my fifties to read John Berger.
Sometimes I think shame is the real source
Of all this. I have no Dickens, zero Proust,
Ditto Tolstoy. I keep being distracted by poems.
I'm a joke. My old tutor, John Chalk,
A Swift expert, turning me on to him and Joyce,
Actually reading *Dubliners* in a lecture
In the hope it would catch fire. ('She was tired.')

    Peter's bushes, home to many sparrows,
Have vanished. Probably for a car space.
I don't blame them. Secretary to no one,
No one is my secretary, except you, empty
Friend. It's possible to see Brexit entirely
As a stationery calamity: no more Rhodia
And Clairefontaine from France, German
Leuchtturm, White Lines from Sweden
And Italian Ciak (chak). Calamity,
Alamity, lamity, amity, mightie, ightie,
Tie, why. Rosen taught me that in a theatre
Of crying children. 'I don't know why.'

I've never needed a reason: language
At full play mixed in with me and silence.
     Forgiveness, have I used you today?
All my clothes are blue or grey.
The youth were here last night.
Their default setting is to shout across
Each other, then, when no one listens,
Shout some more. There is a purple Skittle
Under the sofa. Lord, it's sweet.
Just seen Lawrence in his mafia shades
Though it is November, looking a bit like Hamm,
Playing the ball, not the man of fast increasing sun
This cold day.   Then nothing. Just me, as Krapp said
Into the void (which was the audience).
Ill dreams are the best (not that I am).
Last night I drove across every roundabout
In Italy without signalling. No one even noticed.
You were there when I needed you.
I can never thank you enough.
     Come, Holy Spirit.
And when that other kind came, much harder
To describe, I found you waiting in a corner
Curled up like a dog, happy just to leave the house.
'Chipper,' a colleague called me, which made
It even worse. My tendency to smile while wishing
For the void a mask only three saw through.
I'm not there now, but daily spend time refuting
The pattern that time laid down.   Six and still
Light. I adore the drawing of the blinds
And the lifting of them in the morning to find
The house is still here. You don't have that
In the summer, that sense of discovery
Mixed in with retreat.   I read *Godot* in chapel
With John, Stuart and Jacqui. We weren't angry,
We were bored. As they led us away

Asking why, we said 'Because it was there.'
There are no more conversations,
Only choices about frothed milk and/or syrup.
In case we miss the compulsion to party
We scramble aboard tiny aircraft
To the accompaniment of salsa
While tarmac floods in the gale we have paid
To escape.   Away is no different,
The same confusion reigns, only in strange
Languages, reducing everything to gesture,
Or lack of it, just like our ancestors.
'If I ever go missing, make sure
To use my selfie with the most likes.'
        Now that it is winter I need a new Nordic Noir.
At the end of *Hospital Murders*
After Martin has dumped Gunilla by text,
Gunvald acknowledges Martin's pain,
And Martin confesses his loneliness,
All without uttering a word, monumental,
Beautiful, on a bench at work, the best thing
In the drama by a street, wasted on the credits
passing silently between them.
        Or the Branagh–Wallander Alzheimer's scene:
'Why didn't you tell me? I'm your daughter.'
'Because you're my daughter.'   Six and not light.
We bomb towards darkness at said speed.
That time: do not come for me again.
(Though I think you were there in school.)
Were we all in that room together once?
We were in that room together once.
There is no talking about it, and now
We are in the dark part of the year.
        Bed I had cancer in, bed I broke down in,
Hold me again, now I need you,
Count the minutes with me till dawn,

Pour over me reassurance of your love
While I weep. Sunlight paces the floor
(There is no sunlight).   Call to me,
Was that you calling, don't abandon me.
Sometimes I am more angry than I know.
No one knows this but you, blank *brave*
From France, where they know their paper
Matters. Perfect circumstances, you might say,
For the rational mind to lose its footing.
Have I turned a corner? A storm passes,
And her name with it.   At the back of
Some draughty church a group of boys
Sits giggling as elders low their approval
To the heating fund. I was one of them.
Yet I left with a mysterious belief intact,
Yet different, as Thursday is from Wednesday.
School, I forgive you. You gave me poetry!
Poetry, I forgive you. You gave me friends.
Friends, I salute you for not disappearing
When I threatened to.   The flat Coniston
Water of the future is now a fogged S-bend
Littered with unread tomes. If I go on
Outsourcing my to do list to the internet
I will never keep up. All that's left is breath.
Yet why not not say what happened?
Stairs, why have I come down you? Hallway,
Is there a reason we can invent for me being here?

   Each November a week in bed and a card
From one concerned student. It's a pattern:
I should listen to it. (The week in bed,
Not the card.) At school they told me my
Handwriting was good, but slow. 'He will
Need to speed up to meet the demands
Of the future.' (Story of my life.)
What I want to know is, was I *always* slow,

Or slow because they told me I was?
People tell me it is both beautiful and illegible.
Which came first? My story or theirs?
I don't know much, but this is how we make
Culture.   Late robin, that you sing
Through drear floods my soul with hope.
I hope you know that. I want you to.
Forgiveness, have I used you enough?
Blank paper, Rhodia, my darling Clairefontaine,
So pregnant with promise at the start
Of each day, however terrible my night.
Each year I tell them to buy one of you
So they can change their lives. I should be
On a commission.   Time is running out,
I tell them (it always has) but this way
You notice more, have more ideas
And get to read stationery blogs into the bargain!
What's not to like? I wish Paper Style
Of Sweden exported. A shame the economy
Of generosity hasn't reached them yet.

Speaking of which, heart, how are you?
Not you, my ticker, my *heart*. (By this time
Next week we may have lost The Ashes—
I'll tell you then.) Dark light, blue light,
Paler November than I have seen before,
Stay with me while I shuffle from room
To room calling your name. 'So much
Depends on the red pencil in the orange
Notebook, and which will not come again.'

Cuneiform, panjandrum, malfeasance.
I would like to make your acquaintance
So that I may use you in sentences.
I think of all the greats, sitting with me
On my sick bed, leaning in as I splutter:
Andy, Peter, Chris, Ann, Peter, Ann,

Naomi, Michael, Jean. My audience
Is no bigger. How could it be?
     I want to be in France, with its markets,
The cairns of soap on the tables.
It will be November there, too, the light
Not a patch on this light. The great tit
In the apple tree calls his Pick-you,
Pick-you call. That's always been my problem:
I waited too long to get picked—
By people who didn't even want to pick me.
It's time to stand in a different queue.
Twitter, you blessed me with competitive
Anxiety. Thanks a bunch.   As we spin
Towards dark (with so much light,
With so much light, today!), how are you,
Soul, friend I never dare mention?
I spent a long time trying to thrash you
To sleep, and worse, pretend you weren't there.
'The oil of gladness instead of mourning.'
Yes please. Now all I need is to sit.
And breathe. And breathe.   Such a still
Day. The great thing about illness
Is it teaches you beautiful clarity of thought.
Day, I say yes to you, here, with this notebook,
This pencil, that cost me nothing.
And I would do it all over again, and again,
 Even if no one noticed, even if I never slept again.
'I gave you poetry so you would believe in me.'
And oh, how I did. Do.   Borton, Vickery, Hooper:
The immeasurable joy you have given me.
I cannot thank you enough. To go out and praise,
 Michael once said to me, that's what we do.
We were stuck in traffic at the time,
An ordinary February day.
(It's funny what you remember.)

The light slides from orange, to peach,
To mauve, to lilac, to olive.
Such glory in the dying.
Traffic uses the roads.

Part Four

Bookmark

I have started to use a Bible verse, stuck to cardboard, as a bookmark. Today it slipped between the pages of some prose poems by Jaan Kaplinski I am reading. 'The Lord is a refuge for the oppressed, a stronghold in times of trouble.' It is the kind of thing I would have been given to memorise as a child, as homework for Sunday School, without understanding a word of it.

Signals

On the journey without stopping, my eyelids close without warning. Bad-tempered traffic, a swarm of ill-feeling, each car radiating impatience—without hand signals! I long for the open spaces, those unbroken places where everything, even me, just is: my bones, the clouds, who I was afraid of aged ten, those boys who knew everything, without even putting up their hand to answer. On this dry path I find myself staring into nothing, a cluster of trees. Two lovers emerge, the one leading the other by the hand from shade into further shade where only insects gather. My eyes are dead to the traffic around me. I come to rest, as the voices around me awaken, just so.

The Escape

I end the day where I began it, at a table under a tree googling Mahmoud Darwish. The table is orange, the day scorching. Two men are spending an eternity dismantling an aluminium fire escape with the aid of a small crane. There is only their chatter, the clanging of the swaying steps, one coming to rest on top of another in the bed of their patient truck. I know that trucks are not patient, they are trucks, just as this table is orange and the tree I sit under has a bark of copper, dotted with tiny ants. I found my Darwish article in the end. I had to insert the word 'daughter'. It has not rained for months. The author describes his process of exile, a choice he forced upon his own family. He permitted himself two books from his entire library. A Darwish and a Kibran. His daughter, an avid reader, took only one. 'Tomorrow we will wake up in Chicago.'

After Coucou

A few Septembers ago I missed my uncle's funeral in Switzerland. A year later I broke down completely. I don't know if the two are related. I have a hunch they are. He greeted us with his foghorn voice—*Hell-Oh! How Are You?*—the 'you' performed with an almost inaudible 'i' as in 'ewe'. In his early days a prodigious drinker and smoker, the son of a teetotaller, he won wine-tasting competitions. I adored him. I lay awake once listening to him argue through the wall. He even visited me when I had cancer. To his credit he never remarked on how well I looked, but wanted to know instead how I felt, what had it done to me, who did I think I was now, had I changed?

Wildlife

Rashid invites me for breakfast. It is 10am, and he has been up for hours. 'Yesterday I forget to eat. Today it is different.' He knows I have already eaten, but wants to watch me eat anyway. He sets the plate of lamb and fried onions between us. 'Eat!' he says. 'Please!' He hands me a slice of brown toast which he has torn into perfect halves. He folds a corner around some onion with lamb then dips it into a bowl of cream-coloured tahini. He pronounces this 'tee-hee-nee', like someone trying to suppress a giggle. 'It is delicious, no?' I tell him it is. Propped on the table is his mobile playing a video of a wildlife programme from Sweden. Against a backdrop of rivers and Alaskan-looking forests we watch a group of hunters go about their business in the deep wild. The soundtrack is a plaintive steel guitar. 'I cannot speak Swedish,' not any more. 'I was going there, to be an engineer, but life...My cousins...They needed...I miss them.' He chews again on a large cube of lamb. 'In the spring, my mother would gather the thyme before sunrise, when the day was still cool.' His eyes have dark clouds in them. 'They were *boys*.' He bumps his fists together over his food. 'Please continue,' he says. 'It is most delicious, no?'

Dream Opera

My uncle and cousin are outside in the heat at a large family
wedding. My uncle has lost around four stone and is wearing
his hair in ringlets. Both he and my cousin are very drunk
and can't stop giggling. My mother's here too. She is
unusually loud and gregarious, entertaining everyone with
jokes and singing. During one aria she appears at an upstairs
window, performing to a crowd of us in the garden below.
It is tremendously hot and sticky. It strikes me even as the
dream continues that I rarely dream about my mother.

Part Five

The Names of My Mother

Lise

Bécotte

La Pilule

Lise Françoise Robert

My Love

Mrs J G Wilson

Birdy

(Lisa?)

Aunt Lise

Mrs L F Wilson

Grandmaman

Darling

Mummy

Trying Not to Think of Seamus Heaney

I ease the mower
beneath blackberry stems
and think instead of my mother
who has just called me Angus

stooping to pick a few of the immense dark
planets I try not to think
of my mother already losing
the word for blackberries

who picked blackberries as a child
and took them home to her mother
who knows blackberries
in three languages

each planet of thought
soft between my thumbs
trying not to think
of my mother I think of grass

Bécotte's Poem

I was fast in those days
                                    ooh I was fast
                    the fastest

I won prizes
                    I was the champion

                my father
                                    took me
for chocolate

                                    we drank it
            through whipped cream
                                    oh I was fast

                    our bowls
                    between
                                our   hands

the best feeling

You should have seen me
                                        fearless
                    I was
                                the fastest

No one
                    could catch me

                                            where I am going

                    nothing

Vinaigrette Variations

First take some oil
then some vinegar
one part oil
to one part oil

★

First take some
    it is all about flavouring
        the
then oil

★

You add the vinegar
to the vinegar
when the   vinegar
with the

★

First take the oil
one part
        to
    NO

★

With   then   the
        and
then comes
        the oil

★

and the oil
then the   (?) oil
          the OIL
                  the

Insomnia

Now I no longer sleep
I listen to podcasts of dead poets
and pack for meetings
I already feel I have missed

while my mother roams her house
in a pink dressing gown
swallowing pills calling
Jeffery, is it time yet?

Dear Coffee

I love the way you combine
with bowls and milk
to make breakfast sacred.

Also, you smell fabulous:
one whiff of you is enough
while I gaze at the screen blinking.

You warm my morning pause
with my mother making you for hers,
sucking on a sugar-dipped thumb.

Driving to England

But first was the border road.
Motionless ski-lifts, criss-crossing
the darkness, ascended into blizzard.
The forest shrouded in ghost-light,
the windscreen an emulsion of flakes.

Tapping Telemann on the steering wheel,
my father ignored you kneading
your hands raw, even as we spun
across the lane towards an oncoming
logging truck, making us all ghost.

Morning brought welcome rain, a foretaste
of home, *soup du jour* for breakfast
through truck stop fug, all slurp and cigarettes.
I want to be lost on that road again.
I want you to come with me.

Lament

Four, and lost at Chessington: my earliest memory.
It's all we talk about now, chasing down your memories.

It began in the kitchen: recipes,
tea towels, pots, instructions lost, like memories.

The Christmas we came and cooked for you,
all day you said sorry for losing your memory.

Each day is taken up with such tiny things.
You are playing hide and seek with your memories.

I listen as you call your brother, his voice strong.
'He lost his leg but not his memory!'

Blue cold outside, snow on its way from childhood.
Wrap up warm. Protect what's left of your memories.

Since I knew you, suffering. Your back, your bones,
your breath. Now it's the turn of your memory.

Wherever you are there is laughter.
There also you are. There also are your memories.

What we say now to settle an argument: 'Let's google it.'
'What's Google?' 'It's like never losing your memory.'

We no longer discuss the news. We have each other.
Instead we sit in silence, making peace with our memories.

I love it when you talk about your father.
Everything there is clockwork, a perfect working memory.

By the time you found me I had stopped crying.
'Anthony, you're safe now, I found you.' My earliest memory.

The Four of Us

We are standing by the willow
waiting for the camera to click.
We are all in Sunday best,
though it is a Saturday, trying
not to shiver. It is early May.
There's time enough to argue
who stands where and even
for a joke-shot. Martin took
an hour to choose his tie, another
two to find it. There is banter
about shoulder pads. We've chosen
the frame and the restaurant,
thinking less about posterity
than finding things which fit
and are clean at the exact moment
in history we need to smile together
spontaneously. All of us have hair.

From three gardens away
a lawnmower begins its drone
carving stripes we'll never see.
A woodpigeon clatters above.
The great time we're having
(or had) is not what's really there.
Beyond the silent tripod we have
no idea what lies ahead of us—
futures of wild promise,
snapshots of our own children
under this very willow.
We cannot grasp what we have
been given, or can give back,
except we have chosen to stand
here in close proximity (but not touching),

in pale shirts hoping we will time
our smiles to necessary perfection.
What will stay unspoken
is what we've lost by being here,
those dubious platforms and trysts
we are in the end safer for missing.

The surface of the willow stirs a little
as we wait for Rich to skip
back into line and appear unhurried.
(There is not a time we do not recall
its presence: in summer a miniature
ballroom, in winter a skeleton.)
A magpie, then the Moor Park train.
Then silence. Then a wheezing
and its after-hiss. We become
the record of an adventure
which began far from here with a look
which kept looking, liking what it saw.

Part Six

The Editing Suite

We turn back the film of our lives
        and edit the past in rooms
where no one goes. Those comedy
        childhoods and unthinkable holidays

can all be edited out. The past—those rooms
        we passed through and lived in—
is a childhood or unthinkable holiday
        unspooling in slow-mo black-and-white.

We passed through and lived
        'here,' we say. We prove it with photographs,
which unspool in slow-mo black-and-white
        as we climb the stairs.

'Here,' we say, the proof's in these ones
        of our children, and in those they took
as we climbed the stairs
        or weren't really looking.

Our children we took
        everywhere, passing on love like family jokes
even when we weren't looking,
        perhaps especially then.

Everywhere our love's passed on like family jokes
        which turn back the film of our lives—
perhaps especially then—
        and where no one else can go. Such comedy.

Due

She, due any minute,
pushes the bow-wave
of her body through the gallery
with a waddle, grateful
for the smaller rooms
with benches she unspools
from in slow motion.
He pushes the buggy
containing their child
who does not know
what is about to hit her,
her hair matted and wet.
She cries for a drink
then pushes it away
in disgust. She demands to go free
then pounds the floor
in fury as her father
leans to take her hand.
This may be their final
afternoon together as a three.
The child arches her back,
her tummy and crotch
straining the straps, her feet
dragging deliberately limp.
She asks for another drink,
finishes it in one gulp,
and from nowhere falls asleep.
Briefly two again, they join
hands without a word,
they cannot believe their luck.
The final room is filled
with giant abstracts

(later he will buy one as a poster).
As she makes a beeline for the bench
like an island in the centre,
the child lifts her head
and for one waking moment
takes in the brilliant canvasses,
yells 'Painting!' and, grimacing,
points an accusing finger.

Smoke

We had gone to the woods for blomming.
Eight of us, in our coats, Jamie leading the way.
'Blom, blom, blom, blom, blomming!' we sang,
Twigs cracking, bird-life startling out of bushes
As we marched. Jockie unravelled his knapsack,
And out came the sausages, marshmallows
And frying pan, a page or two of *The Guardian*
For lighting. Quite soon we were weeping,
The smoke slanting through bare trees,
All of us scurrying for twigs while Jockie blew.
Chomping into the sausages we fanned air
Into our mouths, dancing for water.
Marshmallows crinkled and blackened on the embers,
Our stick-ends drooping like rods pulled by salmon
Below water we could not see through,
Nothing said or needing to be said through the smoke
That for days would stay in our eyes,
Our hair, the fabric of our coats,
That would not leave us, however much we rinsed.

My Shyness

Core of my being,
escaping you
was everything.
Throat-lump,
I learned understudy
lines to break your fist
on my tongue
imagining the bliss
of stringing sentences
together in public.
Reading round in French
and Christmas charades
I slayed you finding
I could be anyone.
But first I was nobody
studying the moves
I would never make
and greeting you waiting
on the final night
curtain call, ushered
into the spotlight,
circled, everyone applauding
shouting *Smile!*

For My Children

Now I am no longer any use to you
I wonder how often we will see each other.

Your bags fill the hallway
in exact continuance of your youth.

Of course I will drive you to the station,
you know I cannot refuse you.

I wonder what you will use or remember,
regardless of my instinct to protect you?

Those mornings we sat together,
a book of doodles on the table between us,

your endless requests for biscuits:
I hold them in my fist, a locket nothing will prise open.

Whatever hurt I have caused, I am sorry,
whatever false imaginings, forgive me.

Remember: I did not set out to harm you,
and the mornings were always light,

even when speaking was difficult,
even when you refused my hand.

The Future

My children think they know you
as they prepare statements

to gain entry into the next
of what you have in store.

They return each night
with requests for homework and parties

which bulge indistinguishably in their bags.
Perhaps you look on them kindly

as an uncle they see once a year
slipping them money through his goodbyes.

You place an arm round their shoulders
watching them pay for goods they cannot afford.

You speak to them with kindness,
sending them messages of hope

which pass your lips in silence
even though you are smiling.

Youth

When the youth come to our house
and devour every biscuit,

smearing chocolate chips and crumbs
into our ailing sofa,

and talk without listening over each other,
one of them always asks the big question,

the real question they have come for:
How can I receive the Spirit,

What about suffering,
What about when I doubt?

You are going to be broken,
I want to tell them.

Your friends are going to divorce and disembowel each other.
You are going to have cancer.

You are going to cry out in the wilderness
and no one is going to come to your rescue.

You are going to curse God, the day you were born,
even your parents for having you.

No one is going to want to know you.
Only at that moment will you know

who you really are: your real purpose
will be exposed blinking in raw daylight,

like the war-wounded
wheeled out into the sun. You may never recover.

I also know you are loved.
Let me pray for you.

Boy, Pirouetting

Ovid, Book VIII

Observe this feather falling
    through the draughtless air:

        the plumb line of its spine
            is wrapped in a spinning whorl

        obeying muscle memory
      that's neither flesh nor bone

    and steered by downy barbs
like neurons too small to see.

Still, its stillness turns,
    unspooling its own surprise:

        evidence of gravity,
           not bound by it.

S

          Making a smile,
my lips open,
          making you.

You are the sexiest consonant,
                    enacting your yearning,
     persuasive, insistent, superb
at wet grass,
                    poolside sizzle,
     and mist rising from rivers.

You slink and slide off my tongue.

                    You are sprint and start and sudden,
     coeval with snap but also
surefooted.

S, you slip through me
                    surreptitiously,
     —not a snore, more like
               a shore upon which new waves
                    crash and embellish
     silvering shingle.

You surprise me,
               the first sniff
          in sorry, the final shout
               in yes.

To a Charlie Irvine Guitar Solo

The space
you make
by making each note
grow
in space
between each note
is one I live in

set up my place
of worship
and silently
contemplate
how what is in us
that is made
goes on
being known

by chance
or visitation
that is ecstatic
drunkenness
easeful
and yet studied
sounding natural
cleansed
of information
perfectly
out of time

Poem

Let me invade your heart.
Let me into your hurt
and heal where no one sees.
I place a kiss, here, on your eyes.

(Let me invade your hurt.)
Let me infect where it tears
at you, unseen, in the heart.
Let me dry your eyes.

Let me in. (Your hurt
might burst and invade the world.)
I cradle it, as a baby
crying out in the dark.

Let me. I come as a child
comes, with open hands,
into your dark. To hurt me,
let me invade your heart.

Poem Beginning With a Line by Eve Merriam

I am telling my hands
to be still. They do not want
to be still. My hands are grey,
they are not clean,
they long to be grey again.
There is much they have seen
and cannot speak of.
I have told them
they are beautiful
but they will not listen.
Fidgeting towards silence
is their gift, picking up objects
and placing them back again.
They will not sit
still, joined by hope or nothing
on the dials of old radios, cuttings
from newspapers, pencil-shavings
in a desk-drawer.
My hands gaze up at me with love.
I cannot look at them.
They tell me they are proud
of what I have done.
Do not be afraid, they say,
let us explain to you the truth
of your life: you are loved,
you are more than your hands.

Everything I Know of What I Want to Say

Talking with you I dream into being all I hold precious of
    words I discover
through your finding them in my saying.

When I am with you there is nowhere on earth I flow
    better or am more myself
breathing now with every cell I own.

Take it into your heart that I believe in you fully and taste
    amazing possibility
in the riot of your laughter.

You are enough and are enough and will be enough.
I place you in the light and find you coming into being,
    the world fresh on your shoulders.

You stun me with your hope. It glows in the ache of your
    greeting, your morning eyes
thick with sleep and shining.

Poem of Leaves

I lie down in the leaves,
beneath me the earth.
I pull them over me
like a coat. I disappear
under the leaves
and sink into the earth
where I become one
with the place I am known
whose name has not forgotten
my name, place of rest,
place of leaves melting
into bone, the earth,
this earth, my coat,
with my name in it.

Notes

'Teaching Writing Theory' owes a debt of inspiration to 'In the morning I was presented...' from *Evening Brings Everything Back*, translated by Jaan Kaplinski with Fiona Sampson (Bloodaxe Books, 2004), by Jaan Kaplinski.

'Three Pieces (Poem Beginning with a Line by Yehuda Amichai)' includes a line from 'A Quiet Joy', from *The Selected Poetry of Yehuda Amichai*, translated by Chana Bloch and Stephen Mitchell (University of California Press, 1996), by Yehuda Amichai.

'The Barchester Chronicles' is for Michael Symmons Roberts, whose adaptations of Trollope for BBC radio the poem refers to. The poem also makes reference to the television adaptation of *The History Man* by Malcolm Bradbury. The final line of the poem quotes from the novel of the same name.

'Poem Beginning With a Line by John Ash' includes a line from 'Partial Explanation', from *In the Wake of the Day* (Carcanet, 2010), by John Ash; the poem also quotes from 'In Earliest Morning', from *Collected Poems* (Farrar, Straus and Giroux, 1993), by James Schuyler.

'To a Notebook' quotes from: 'Sketch for Dawn' from the album *LC* (Factory Records, 1981), by The Durutti Column; 'Si' from the album *Honey and Wine* (LeeTatiana Music, 1989), by Sublime; *The Undefended Life* (Human Ecology Partners, 2009) by Simon Walker; 'A Few Days' from *Collected Poems* (Farrar, Straus and Giroux, 1993) by James Schuyler; *One Minute Mindfulness* by Simon Parke (Hay House, 2011). 'God comes to you disguised as your life' is a line by Paula D'Arcy.

'Poem Beginning With a Line by Eve Merriam' includes a line from 'New Love', from *The Place My Words Are Looking For*, edited by Paul B. Janeczko (Bradbury Press, 1990), by Eve Merriam.

'To Spring' is for John Bryant; 'Thinking Outside' is for Daniel Pacey; 'Staffroom, Summer, 2015' is for Helen Bradford; 'British Teeth' is for Cliff Yates; 'Chicken and Almond Soup' is for Margo Greenwood; 'Smoke' is for Jamie Encombe; 'The Four of Us' is for my mother and father.

Acknowledgements

Grateful thanks are due to the editors of the following publications where these poems, or earlier versions of them, first appeared: Aerodrome, And Other Poems, Antiphon, Hinterland, Ink Sweat & Tears, The Interpreter's House, London Grip New Poetry, The North, The Rialto, Riptide, Under the Radar.

'Three Pieces (Poem Beginning with a Line by Yehuda Amichai)' appeared in *Hands and Wings: Poems for Freedom From Torture*, edited by Dorothy McCarthy (White Rat Press, 2015).

'To Spring' was published in *With You In Mind*, an online anthology in support of Mental Health Awareness Week 2015, curated by Sarah James at sarah-james.co.uk.

'From a Chalkface' was commissioned by Michael McKimm and appeared in *Map: Poems After William Smith's Map of 1815* (Worple Press, 2015).

'My Shyness' was published in *Wenlock Poetry Festival 2015*, edited by Nadia Kingsley (Fair Acre Press, 2015).

'Boy, Pirouetting' is for Paddy Randall, was commissioned by Nessa O'Mahony and Paul Munden, and appeared in *Metamorphic: 21st Century Poets Respond to Ovid* (Fresh Work Press, 2017).

'Poem' was published in *Poems for Children's Heart Week*, curated by Rebecca Gross at rebeccagoss.wordpress.com.

'Everything I Know of What I Want to Say' was published at simonparke.com.

'On Losing the Ability to Sleep', 'Due', 'The Editing Suite', 'To a Charlie Irvine Guitar Solo' and 'Poem Beginning With a Line by Eve Merriam', appeared in *Lyrical: A small book of poems* (Lulu, 2014), edited by Martin Wroe. 'The Editing Suite' is for Crispin Holland.

'Poem of Leaves' was commissioned by Michael McKimm and appeared in *The Tree Line: Poems for Trees, Woods & People* (Worple Press, 2017).

Poems in this collection were shortlisted in the 2016/17 Poetry Business International Book and Pamphlet Competition.

I am grateful to Michael Bartholomew-Biggs, Andy Brown, Peter Carpenter, Naomi Jaffa, Peter Sansom and Christopher Southgate for their comments on poems in this collection.